50 Hot Sauce Recipes for Home

By: Kelly Johnson

Table of Contents

- Classic Tabasco-Style Hot Sauce
- Sriracha Sauce
- Habanero Hot Sauce
- Jalapeño Hot Sauce
- Chipotle Hot Sauce
- Ghost Pepper Hot Sauce
- Pineapple Habanero Hot Sauce
- Garlic Hot Sauce
- Roasted Red Pepper Hot Sauce
- Green Chili Hot Sauce
- Mango Habanero Hot Sauce
- Sweet Chili Hot Sauce
- Smoky Chipotle Hot Sauce
- Thai Chili Hot Sauce
- Fermented Hot Sauce
- Cayenne Pepper Hot Sauce
- Asian-Style Hot Sauce
- Scorpion Pepper Hot Sauce
- Spicy Garlic Sauce
- Carrot Hot Sauce
- Cilantro Lime Hot Sauce
- Bourbon Hot Sauce
- Tomato-Based Hot Sauce
- Blueberry Hot Sauce
- Watermelon Jalapeño Hot Sauce
- Apricot Hot Sauce
- Roasted Garlic and Herb Hot Sauce
- Blackberry Habanero Hot Sauce
- Chipotle Pineapple Hot Sauce
- Fire Roasted Salsa Verde
- Caramelized Onion Hot Sauce
- Lemon Basil Hot Sauce
- Zesty Avocado Hot Sauce
- Apple Cider Hot Sauce
- Spicy Peach Hot Sauce

- Raspberry Chipotle Hot Sauce
- Tomato and Garlic Hot Sauce
- Cucumber Jalapeño Hot Sauce
- Sweet and Spicy Hot Sauce
- Avocado Green Hot Sauce
- Ginger Hot Sauce
- Dill Pickle Hot Sauce
- Citrus Hot Sauce
- Cherry Habanero Hot Sauce
- Spicy Honey Hot Sauce
- Smoked Paprika Hot Sauce
- Curry Hot Sauce
- Cranberry Hot Sauce
- Tomato and Mango Hot Sauce
- Honey Garlic Hot Sauce

Classic Tabasco-Style Hot Sauce

Ingredients:

- 2 cups tabasco peppers, stems removed
- 1 cup white vinegar
- 1 teaspoon salt

Instructions:

1. **Blend the Peppers**
   In a blender, combine tabasco peppers, vinegar, and salt. Blend until smooth.
2. **Strain the Mixture**
   Pour the mixture through a fine-mesh sieve into a bowl, pressing down to extract the liquid.
3. **Ferment**
   Transfer the liquid to a sterilized bottle and let it ferment at room temperature for about 2-3 weeks.
4. **Store**
   Once fermented, transfer to the refrigerator and use as desired.

Sriracha Sauce

Ingredients:

- 1 cup red jalapeño peppers, stems removed
- 1/2 cup garlic, minced
- 1/4 cup sugar
- 1/2 cup white vinegar
- 1 teaspoon salt

Instructions:

1. **Blend the Peppers and Garlic**
   In a blender, combine red jalapeños, garlic, sugar, vinegar, and salt. Blend until smooth.
2. **Cook the Mixture**
   Pour the mixture into a saucepan and simmer over low heat for about 10-15 minutes.
3. **Cool and Store**
   Let cool, then transfer to a bottle and refrigerate.

Habanero Hot Sauce

Ingredients:

- 1 cup habanero peppers, stems removed
- 1 cup white vinegar
- 1/2 cup carrot, chopped
- 1 teaspoon salt

Instructions:

1. **Blend the Ingredients**
   In a blender, combine habaneros, vinegar, carrots, and salt. Blend until smooth.
2. **Cook the Mixture**
   Pour the mixture into a saucepan and bring to a boil. Simmer for 10 minutes.
3. **Cool and Store**
   Let cool, then transfer to a bottle and refrigerate.

Jalapeño Hot Sauce

Ingredients:

- 1 cup jalapeño peppers, stems removed
- 1/2 cup white vinegar
- 1 tablespoon garlic, minced
- 1 teaspoon salt

Instructions:

1. **Blend the Ingredients**
   In a blender, combine jalapeños, vinegar, garlic, and salt. Blend until smooth.
2. **Cook the Mixture**
   Pour the mixture into a saucepan and simmer over low heat for about 10 minutes.
3. **Cool and Store**
   Let cool, then transfer to a bottle and refrigerate.

Chipotle Hot Sauce

Ingredients:

- 1 cup chipotle peppers in adobo sauce
- 1/2 cup white vinegar
- 1 teaspoon salt
- 1 teaspoon sugar

Instructions:

1. **Blend the Ingredients**
   In a blender, combine chipotle peppers, vinegar, salt, and sugar. Blend until smooth.
2. **Store**
   Transfer to a bottle and refrigerate.

Ghost Pepper Hot Sauce

Ingredients:

- 1 cup ghost peppers, stems removed
- 1/2 cup white vinegar
- 1/4 cup garlic, minced
- 1 teaspoon salt

Instructions:

1. **Blend the Ingredients**
   In a blender, combine ghost peppers, vinegar, garlic, and salt. Blend until smooth.
2. **Cook the Mixture**
   Pour the mixture into a saucepan and simmer for about 10 minutes.
3. **Cool and Store**
   Let cool, then transfer to a bottle and refrigerate.

Pineapple Habanero Hot Sauce

Ingredients:

- 1 cup fresh pineapple, chopped
- 1/2 cup habanero peppers, stems removed
- 1/2 cup white vinegar
- 1 teaspoon salt

Instructions:

1. **Blend the Ingredients**
   In a blender, combine pineapple, habaneros, vinegar, and salt. Blend until smooth.
2. **Cook the Mixture**
   Pour the mixture into a saucepan and simmer for about 10-15 minutes.
3. **Cool and Store**
   Let cool, then transfer to a bottle and refrigerate.

Garlic Hot Sauce

Ingredients:

- 1 cup garlic cloves
- 1 cup white vinegar
- 1 teaspoon salt

Instructions:

1. **Blend the Ingredients**
   In a blender, combine garlic, vinegar, and salt. Blend until smooth.
2. **Cook the Mixture**
   Pour the mixture into a saucepan and simmer for about 10-15 minutes.
3. **Cool and Store**
   Let cool, then transfer to a bottle and refrigerate.

Roasted Red Pepper Hot Sauce

Ingredients:

- 2 cups roasted red peppers, peeled and seeded
- 1/2 cup white vinegar
- 1 tablespoon olive oil
- 1 teaspoon salt
- 1 teaspoon sugar

Instructions:

1. **Blend the Ingredients**
   In a blender, combine roasted red peppers, vinegar, olive oil, salt, and sugar. Blend until smooth.
2. **Store**
   Transfer to a bottle and refrigerate.

Green Chili Hot Sauce

Ingredients:

- 1 cup green chili peppers, stems removed
- 1/2 cup white vinegar
- 1 tablespoon garlic, minced
- 1 teaspoon salt

Instructions:

1. **Blend the Ingredients**
   In a blender, combine green chilies, vinegar, garlic, and salt. Blend until smooth.
2. **Cook the Mixture**
   Pour the mixture into a saucepan and simmer for about 10 minutes.
3. **Cool and Store**
   Let cool, then transfer to a bottle and refrigerate.

Mango Habanero Hot Sauce

Ingredients:

- 1 cup mango, chopped
- 1/2 cup habanero peppers, stems removed
- 1/2 cup white vinegar
- 1 teaspoon salt

Instructions:

1. **Blend the Ingredients**
   In a blender, combine mango, habaneros, vinegar, and salt. Blend until smooth.
2. **Cook the Mixture**
   Pour the mixture into a saucepan and simmer for about 10 minutes.
3. **Cool and Store**
   Let cool, then transfer to a bottle and refrigerate.

Sweet Chili Hot Sauce

Ingredients:

- 1 cup red chili peppers, stems removed
- 1/2 cup sugar
- 1/2 cup white vinegar
- 1 teaspoon garlic, minced

Instructions:

1. **Blend the Ingredients**
   In a blender, combine red chilies, sugar, vinegar, and garlic. Blend until smooth.
2. **Cook the Mixture**
   Pour the mixture into a saucepan and simmer for about 10 minutes.
3. **Cool and Store**
   Let cool, then transfer to a bottle and refrigerate.

Smoky Chipotle Hot Sauce

Ingredients:

- 1 cup chipotle peppers in adobo sauce
- 1/2 cup white vinegar
- 1 teaspoon smoked paprika
- 1 teaspoon salt

Instructions:

1. **Blend the Ingredients**
   In a blender, combine chipotle peppers, vinegar, smoked paprika, and salt. Blend until smooth.
2. **Store**
   Transfer to a bottle and refrigerate.

Thai Chili Hot Sauce

Ingredients:

- 1 cup Thai bird's eye chilies, stems removed
- 1/2 cup white vinegar
- 1 tablespoon garlic, minced
- 1 teaspoon salt

Instructions:

1. **Blend the Ingredients**
   In a blender, combine bird's eye chilies, vinegar, garlic, and salt. Blend until smooth.
2. **Cook the Mixture**
   Pour the mixture into a saucepan and simmer for about 10 minutes.
3. **Cool and Store**
   Let cool, then transfer to a bottle and refrigerate.

Fermented Hot Sauce

Ingredients:

- 2 cups hot peppers, stems removed
- 1/2 cup water
- 1 tablespoon salt

Instructions:

1. **Combine Ingredients**
   In a jar, combine hot peppers, water, and salt. Stir to dissolve the salt.
2. **Ferment**
   Cover the jar with a cloth and let it ferment at room temperature for 1-2 weeks, stirring occasionally.
3. **Blend and Store**
   After fermentation, blend the mixture until smooth and transfer to a bottle. Refrigerate.

Cayenne Pepper Hot Sauce

Ingredients:

- 1 cup cayenne peppers, stems removed
- 1/2 cup white vinegar
- 1 teaspoon garlic, minced
- 1 teaspoon salt

Instructions:

1. **Blend the Ingredients**
   In a blender, combine cayenne peppers, vinegar, garlic, and salt. Blend until smooth.
2. **Cook the Mixture**
   Pour the mixture into a saucepan and simmer for about 10 minutes.
3. **Cool and Store**
   Let cool, then transfer to a bottle and refrigerate.

Asian-Style Hot Sauce

Ingredients:

- 1 cup red chili peppers, stems removed
- 1/2 cup rice vinegar
- 2 tablespoons soy sauce
- 1 tablespoon sesame oil
- 1 teaspoon garlic, minced

Instructions:

1. **Blend the Ingredients**
   In a blender, combine red chili peppers, rice vinegar, soy sauce, sesame oil, and garlic. Blend until smooth.
2. **Store**
   Transfer to a bottle and refrigerate.

Scorpion Pepper Hot Sauce

Ingredients:

- 1 cup scorpion peppers, stems removed
- 1/2 cup white vinegar
- 1 tablespoon salt
- 1 tablespoon lime juice

Instructions:

1. **Blend the Ingredients**
   In a blender, combine scorpion peppers, vinegar, salt, and lime juice. Blend until smooth.
2. **Cook the Mixture**
   Pour the mixture into a saucepan and simmer for about 10 minutes.
3. **Cool and Store**
   Let cool, then transfer to a bottle and refrigerate.

Spicy Garlic Sauce

Ingredients:

- 1 cup chili garlic sauce
- 1/2 cup soy sauce
- 2 tablespoons sugar
- 1 tablespoon rice vinegar

Instructions:

1. **Mix the Ingredients**
   In a bowl, combine chili garlic sauce, soy sauce, sugar, and rice vinegar.
2. **Store**
   Transfer to a bottle and refrigerate.

Carrot Hot Sauce

Ingredients:

- 1 cup carrots, peeled and chopped
- 1/2 cup white vinegar
- 1 tablespoon habanero peppers, chopped
- 1 teaspoon salt

Instructions:

1. **Blend the Ingredients**
   In a blender, combine carrots, vinegar, habanero peppers, and salt. Blend until smooth.
2. **Cook the Mixture**
   Pour the mixture into a saucepan and simmer for about 10 minutes.
3. **Cool and Store**
   Let cool, then transfer to a bottle and refrigerate.

Cilantro Lime Hot Sauce

Ingredients:

- 1 cup cilantro, chopped
- 1/2 cup lime juice
- 1 tablespoon jalapeño peppers, chopped
- 1 teaspoon salt

Instructions:

1. **Blend the Ingredients**
   In a blender, combine cilantro, lime juice, jalapeños, and salt. Blend until smooth.
2. **Store**
   Transfer to a bottle and refrigerate.

Bourbon Hot Sauce

Ingredients:

- 1 cup hot peppers, stems removed
- 1/2 cup bourbon
- 1/2 cup white vinegar
- 1 tablespoon garlic, minced

Instructions:

1. **Blend the Ingredients**
   In a blender, combine hot peppers, bourbon, vinegar, and garlic. Blend until smooth.
2. **Cook the Mixture**
   Pour the mixture into a saucepan and simmer for about 10 minutes.
3. **Cool and Store**
   Let cool, then transfer to a bottle and refrigerate.

Tomato-Based Hot Sauce

Ingredients:

- 2 cups tomatoes, chopped
- 1/2 cup white vinegar
- 1 tablespoon red chili flakes
- 1 teaspoon salt

Instructions:

1. **Blend the Ingredients**
   In a blender, combine tomatoes, vinegar, red chili flakes, and salt. Blend until smooth.
2. **Cook the Mixture**
   Pour the mixture into a saucepan and simmer for about 15 minutes.
3. **Cool and Store**
   Let cool, then transfer to a bottle and refrigerate.

Blueberry Hot Sauce

Ingredients:

- 1 cup blueberries, fresh or frozen
- 1/2 cup white vinegar
- 1 tablespoon jalapeño peppers, chopped
- 1 tablespoon honey

Instructions:

1. **Blend the Ingredients**
   In a blender, combine blueberries, vinegar, jalapeños, and honey. Blend until smooth.
2. **Cook the Mixture**
   Pour the mixture into a saucepan and simmer for about 10 minutes.
3. **Cool and Store**
   Let cool, then transfer to a bottle and refrigerate.

Watermelon Jalapeño Hot Sauce

Ingredients:

- 2 cups watermelon, cubed
- 1/2 cup jalapeño peppers, chopped
- 1/2 cup white vinegar
- 1 tablespoon lime juice
- 1 teaspoon salt

Instructions:

1. **Blend the Ingredients**
   In a blender, combine watermelon, jalapeños, vinegar, lime juice, and salt. Blend until smooth.
2. **Store**
   Transfer to a bottle and refrigerate.

Apricot Hot Sauce

Ingredients:

- 2 cups apricots, pitted and chopped
- 1/2 cup white vinegar
- 1 tablespoon habanero peppers, chopped
- 1 teaspoon salt

Instructions:

1. **Blend the Ingredients**
   In a blender, combine apricots, vinegar, habaneros, and salt. Blend until smooth.
2. **Cook the Mixture**
   Pour the mixture into a saucepan and simmer for about 10 minutes.
3. **Cool and Store**
   Let cool, then transfer to a bottle and refrigerate.

Roasted Garlic and Herb Hot Sauce

Ingredients:

- 1 head garlic, roasted
- 1/2 cup white vinegar
- 1/2 cup fresh herbs (like basil, thyme, or parsley)
- 1 tablespoon chili flakes
- 1 teaspoon salt

Instructions:

1. **Blend the Ingredients**
   In a blender, combine roasted garlic, vinegar, herbs, chili flakes, and salt. Blend until smooth.
2. **Store**
   Transfer to a bottle and refrigerate.

Blackberry Habanero Hot Sauce

Ingredients:

- 2 cups blackberries, fresh or frozen
- 1/2 cup white vinegar
- 1 tablespoon habanero peppers, chopped
- 1 teaspoon sugar

Instructions:

1. **Blend the Ingredients**
   In a blender, combine blackberries, vinegar, habaneros, and sugar. Blend until smooth.
2. **Cook the Mixture**
   Pour the mixture into a saucepan and simmer for about 10 minutes.
3. **Cool and Store**
   Let cool, then transfer to a bottle and refrigerate.

Chipotle Pineapple Hot Sauce

Ingredients:

- 1 cup pineapple, diced
- 1/2 cup chipotle peppers in adobo sauce
- 1/2 cup white vinegar
- 1 tablespoon lime juice

Instructions:

1. **Blend the Ingredients**
   In a blender, combine pineapple, chipotle peppers, vinegar, and lime juice. Blend until smooth.
2. **Store**
   Transfer to a bottle and refrigerate.

Fire Roasted Salsa Verde

Ingredients:

- 2 cups tomatillos, husked and chopped
- 1/2 cup onions, chopped
- 1/4 cup cilantro, chopped
- 1 jalapeño, chopped
- 1/2 cup lime juice

Instructions:

1. **Roast the Ingredients**
   Roast tomatillos, onions, and jalapeños on a baking sheet at 400°F (200°C) for about 15 minutes.
2. **Blend the Mixture**
   In a blender, combine roasted ingredients, cilantro, and lime juice. Blend until smooth.
3. **Store**
   Transfer to a bottle and refrigerate.

Caramelized Onion Hot Sauce

Ingredients:

- 2 cups onions, thinly sliced
- 1/2 cup white vinegar
- 1/4 cup chili flakes
- 1 tablespoon olive oil
- 1 teaspoon salt

Instructions:

1. **Caramelize the Onions**
   In a skillet, heat olive oil over medium heat and add onions. Cook until caramelized (about 20 minutes).
2. **Blend the Mixture**
   In a blender, combine caramelized onions, vinegar, chili flakes, and salt. Blend until smooth.
3. **Store**
   Transfer to a bottle and refrigerate.

Lemon Basil Hot Sauce

Ingredients:

- 1 cup fresh basil leaves
- 1/2 cup lemon juice
- 1/4 cup white vinegar
- 1 tablespoon jalapeño peppers, chopped
- 1 teaspoon salt

Instructions:

1. **Blend the Ingredients**
   In a blender, combine basil, lemon juice, vinegar, jalapeños, and salt. Blend until smooth.
2. **Store**
   Transfer to a bottle and refrigerate.

Zesty Avocado Hot Sauce

Ingredients:

- 2 ripe avocados, peeled and pitted
- 1/2 cup lime juice
- 1/2 cup cilantro, chopped
- 1 jalapeño, chopped
- 1/4 cup water
- 1 teaspoon salt

Instructions:

1. **Blend the Ingredients**
   In a blender, combine avocados, lime juice, cilantro, jalapeño, water, and salt. Blend until smooth.
2. **Store**
   Transfer to a bottle and refrigerate.

Apple Cider Hot Sauce

Ingredients:

- 1 cup apple cider vinegar
- 1/2 cup jalapeño peppers, chopped
- 1/2 cup apple sauce
- 1 tablespoon honey
- 1 teaspoon salt

Instructions:

1. **Blend the Ingredients**
   In a blender, combine apple cider vinegar, jalapeños, apple sauce, honey, and salt. Blend until smooth.
2. **Store**
   Transfer to a bottle and refrigerate.

Spicy Peach Hot Sauce

Ingredients:

- 2 cups peaches, pitted and chopped
- 1/2 cup white vinegar
- 1/2 cup habanero peppers, chopped
- 1 tablespoon lime juice
- 1 teaspoon salt

Instructions:

1. **Blend the Ingredients**
   In a blender, combine peaches, vinegar, habaneros, lime juice, and salt. Blend until smooth.
2. **Cook the Mixture**
   Pour the mixture into a saucepan and simmer for about 10 minutes.
3. **Cool and Store**
   Let cool, then transfer to a bottle and refrigerate.

Raspberry Chipotle Hot Sauce

Ingredients:

- 2 cups raspberries, fresh or frozen
- 1/2 cup chipotle peppers in adobo sauce
- 1/2 cup white vinegar
- 1 tablespoon honey

Instructions:

1. **Blend the Ingredients**
   In a blender, combine raspberries, chipotle peppers, vinegar, and honey. Blend until smooth.
2. **Cook the Mixture**
   Pour the mixture into a saucepan and simmer for about 10 minutes.
3. **Cool and Store**
   Let cool, then transfer to a bottle and refrigerate.

Tomato and Garlic Hot Sauce

Ingredients:

- 2 cups tomatoes, chopped
- 1 head garlic, roasted
- 1/2 cup white vinegar
- 1 teaspoon chili flakes
- 1 teaspoon salt

Instructions:

1. **Blend the Ingredients**
   In a blender, combine tomatoes, roasted garlic, vinegar, chili flakes, and salt. Blend until smooth.
2. **Store**
   Transfer to a bottle and refrigerate.

Cucumber Jalapeño Hot Sauce

Ingredients:

- 2 cups cucumber, peeled and chopped
- 1/2 cup jalapeño peppers, chopped
- 1/2 cup white vinegar
- 1 tablespoon lime juice
- 1 teaspoon salt

Instructions:

1. **Blend the Ingredients**
   In a blender, combine cucumber, jalapeños, vinegar, lime juice, and salt. Blend until smooth.
2. **Store**
   Transfer to a bottle and refrigerate.

Sweet and Spicy Hot Sauce

Ingredients:

- 1 cup mango, chopped
- 1/2 cup white vinegar
- 1/2 cup habanero peppers, chopped
- 1 tablespoon honey
- 1 teaspoon salt

Instructions:

1. **Blend the Ingredients**
   In a blender, combine mango, vinegar, habaneros, honey, and salt. Blend until smooth.
2. **Cook the Mixture**
   Pour the mixture into a saucepan and simmer for about 10 minutes.
3. **Cool and Store**
   Let cool, then transfer to a bottle and refrigerate.

Avocado Green Hot Sauce

Ingredients:

- 2 ripe avocados, peeled and pitted
- 1/2 cup lime juice
- 1/2 cup cilantro, chopped
- 1 jalapeño, chopped
- 1/4 cup water
- 1 teaspoon salt

Instructions:

1. **Blend the Ingredients**
   In a blender, combine avocados, lime juice, cilantro, jalapeño, water, and salt. Blend until smooth.
2. **Store**
   Transfer to a bottle and refrigerate.

Ginger Hot Sauce

Ingredients:

- 1 cup fresh ginger, peeled and chopped
- 1/2 cup white vinegar
- 1/2 cup water
- 1/4 cup honey
- 1 teaspoon salt

Instructions:

1. **Blend the Ingredients**
   In a blender, combine ginger, vinegar, water, honey, and salt. Blend until smooth.
2. **Store**
   Transfer to a bottle and refrigerate.

Dill Pickle Hot Sauce

Ingredients:

- 1 cup dill pickles, chopped
- 1/2 cup pickle juice
- 1/2 cup white vinegar
- 1 teaspoon cayenne pepper
- 1 teaspoon garlic powder

Instructions:

1. **Blend the Ingredients**
   In a blender, combine dill pickles, pickle juice, vinegar, cayenne, and garlic powder. Blend until smooth.
2. **Store**
   Transfer to a bottle and refrigerate.

Citrus Hot Sauce

Ingredients:

- 1 cup citrus juice (orange, lemon, or lime)
- 1/2 cup white vinegar
- 1/2 cup habanero peppers, chopped
- 1 teaspoon salt

Instructions:

1. **Blend the Ingredients**
   In a blender, combine citrus juice, vinegar, habaneros, and salt. Blend until smooth.
2. **Store**
   Transfer to a bottle and refrigerate.

Cherry Habanero Hot Sauce

Ingredients:

- 2 cups cherries, pitted and chopped
- 1/2 cup habanero peppers, chopped
- 1/2 cup white vinegar
- 1 tablespoon honey

Instructions:

1. **Blend the Ingredients**
   In a blender, combine cherries, habaneros, vinegar, and honey. Blend until smooth.
2. **Cook the Mixture**
   Pour the mixture into a saucepan and simmer for about 10 minutes.
3. **Cool and Store**
   Let cool, then transfer to a bottle and refrigerate.

Spicy Honey Hot Sauce

Ingredients:

- 1 cup honey
- 1/2 cup red chili flakes
- 1/4 cup white vinegar
- 1 teaspoon garlic powder

Instructions:

1. **Combine the Ingredients**
   In a saucepan, combine honey, chili flakes, vinegar, and garlic powder.
2. **Heat the Mixture**
   Heat over low heat until warmed through.
3. **Cool and Store**
   Let cool, then transfer to a bottle and refrigerate.

Smoked Paprika Hot Sauce

Ingredients:

- 1 cup smoked paprika
- 1/2 cup white vinegar
- 1/2 cup water
- 1 teaspoon cayenne pepper
- 1 teaspoon salt

Instructions:

1. **Blend the Ingredients**
   In a blender, combine smoked paprika, vinegar, water, cayenne, and salt. Blend until smooth.
2. **Store**
   Transfer to a bottle and refrigerate.

Curry Hot Sauce

Ingredients:

- 1 cup coconut milk
- 1/2 cup curry powder
- 1/2 cup white vinegar
- 1/2 cup jalapeño peppers, chopped

Instructions:

1. **Blend the Ingredients**
   In a blender, combine coconut milk, curry powder, vinegar, and jalapeños. Blend until smooth.
2. **Cook the Mixture**
   Pour the mixture into a saucepan and simmer for about 10 minutes.
3. **Cool and Store**
   Let cool, then transfer to a bottle and refrigerate.

Cranberry Hot Sauce

Ingredients:

- 2 cups fresh cranberries
- 1/2 cup white vinegar
- 1/2 cup sugar
- 1/4 cup jalapeño peppers, chopped

Instructions:

1. **Blend the Ingredients**
   In a blender, combine cranberries, vinegar, sugar, and jalapeños. Blend until smooth.
2. **Cook the Mixture**
   Pour the mixture into a saucepan and simmer for about 10 minutes.
3. **Cool and Store**
   Let cool, then transfer to a bottle and refrigerate.

Tomato and Mango Hot Sauce

Ingredients:

- 2 ripe tomatoes, chopped
- 1 ripe mango, peeled and diced
- 1/2 cup white vinegar
- 1/4 cup onion, chopped
- 2 cloves garlic, minced
- 1 teaspoon salt
- 1 teaspoon cayenne pepper

Instructions:

1. **Blend the Ingredients**
   In a blender, combine tomatoes, mango, vinegar, onion, garlic, salt, and cayenne pepper. Blend until smooth.
2. **Cook the Mixture**
   Pour the mixture into a saucepan and simmer for about 15 minutes, stirring occasionally.
3. **Cool and Store**
   Let cool, then transfer to a bottle and refrigerate.

Honey Garlic Hot Sauce

Ingredients:

- 1/2 cup honey
- 1/2 cup white vinegar
- 4 cloves garlic, minced
- 1/4 cup chili flakes
- 1 teaspoon salt

Instructions:

1. **Combine the Ingredients**
   In a saucepan, combine honey, vinegar, garlic, chili flakes, and salt.
2. **Heat the Mixture**
   Heat over low heat until warmed through, stirring occasionally.
3. **Cool and Store**
   Let cool, then transfer to a bottle and refrigerate.